Carry On

Carry On

Let There Be Light

Inspirations by

JOAN STONE

Carry On, Let There Be Light

Copyright © 2019 by Joan Stone. All rights reserved.

No part of this publication may be reproduced, stored in a retrieval system or transmitted in any way by any means, electronic, mechanical, photocopy, recording or otherwise without the prior permission of the author except as provided by USA copyright law.

The opinions expressed by the author are not necessarily those of URLink Print and Media.

1603 Capitol Ave., Suite 310 Cheyenne, Wyoming USA 82001
1-888-980-6523 | admin@urlinkpublishing.com

URLink Print and Media is committed to excellence in the publishing industry.

Book design copyright © 2019 by URLink Print and Media. All rights reserved.

Published in the United States of America
ISBN 978-1-64367-378-3 (Paperback)
ISBN 978-1-64367-377-6 (Digital)

03.05.19

List of Poems

The Mirror

My Gracious God

My Eyes Wide Open

Free

Beautiful World

Let it out..

The Journey

Look Inside

Friends

God's Will

Growing Faith

Open Up

Live To Be Free

You Will Get Through

True To You

Go For It

Pain

Thoughts

Who You Were

The RollerCoaster

Feelings

To Let Go

Surrender

Wait

Get Over It

Always Be Grateful

Direction

The Past

Ride The Wave

Humble

Finding Me

Determination

Insanity

Vision of Me

More Revealed

The Road

The Mirror

In my room, stands a mirror.
Shiny, beautiful, but reflecting fear.

When I stand in front of it, what do I see?
An empty lonely person, staring back at me.

Filled with sorrow, filled with pain.
Truth be told, I was going insane.

Then one day, I opened my eyes.
Got out of bed, to a wonderful surprise.

I could change, the person I see.
To someone who cares, to someone to be free.

Looking through the years, where had I lost control.
It's clear to me now, they had taken my soul.

I can be, who I want to be.
For God's in my life, looking after me.

I need to stand tall, stand back, breathe and see.
That I am exactly, where I am meant to be.

My Gracious God

Today is the first day, of the rest of my life.
The journey to get here, was not all a delight.

Worried about the future, dwelling on the past.
Made unsettled feelings, and stirred up emotions last.

When all along, I had to learn.
To live for today, so God I did turn.

My faith grows stronger, when I allow God in.
No sense in fighting, a battle I cannot win.

So with love and support, I have found the way.
To let it all go. It's simple, pray.

I try too hard to change, the way my life is.
I just need to stand back, and let God make it his.

I am right where, I am suppose to be.
With my gracious God, watching over me.

My Eyes Wide Open

I opened my eyes, and what did I see?
A whole new world, staring back me.

So many places, so many things.
I opened my eyes, to what it all brings.

So much to see, so much to do too.
Letting it slip away, is the worst I could do.

It's one foot forward, in front of me.
To be the person, I am meant to be.

Only I, can make this change.
For what I seek, is still in range.

Open my eyes, open my heart.
For the world to adhere, to my fresh new start!

Free

A part inside, needed setting free.
So I decided, to look for me.

What I found, was scary but true.
My ongoing troubles, they were the clue.

Why had my life, not made sense?
As I seemed to be, always sitting on the fence.

I allowed my head, to be clouded and torn.
Causing my heart, to be tired and worn.

When all along, for me to be free.
The place to look, was deep inside of me.

So I dug deep, and what I found.
Was a new attitude, and a voice with sound.

The only way, for me to be free.
Was to change my life, to start caring for me.

So if you're lost, given up on all.
Changing your attitude, will answer the call.

Beautiful World

When I walk alone, that's when I see,
What this wonderful world, has to offer me.

The glory, the beauty, the grace of it all
Whether it's big, or whether it's small.

A bird in the sky, or a bumblebee
That's the feeling, of being free.

Take nothing for granted, and see the light.
Remember the world, is a beautiful sight.

Let it out..

There is a dark place, where we hold pain and fear inside,
Until we realize, we can no longer run and hide.

But all the pain, and fear within,
Closed your heart, and set your mind in a spin.

Comes a time in life, when you must open the door.
Letting it flow out, until you hurt no more.

Instead of trying, to push it away,
Take time to sit, and quietly pray.

So let go of all, your pain and fear.
Surrender to God, as he's always near.

Hold onto your life, let it all out.
God is here, go ahead and shout.

The Journey

The life I lived in the past, and my life today.
Are so unbelievably different, but what a journey along the way.

A journey with moments, of sadness and despair.
Where I forgot how to love, where I forgot how to care.

I knew the way, to get out of this space.
But my stubbornness, kept staring me in the face.

It was a game, where I would always hide.
Never listening, to the whispers inside.

It was so simple, if I would just let go.
The answers come, sometime fast, sometimes slow.

I could be strong, happy and free.
The only one stopping this…. was me!

Look Inside

If we could be, as free as a bird.
If we could grasp, our every word.

To give us hope, strength and power.
To imagine the rain, as a wonderful shower.

To have the courage, to handle it all,
Whether it be big, or whether it be small.

Why hold it inside, we need just open the door.
To a life of fulfilled promises, and a whole lot more.

Friends

Friends are there, to help you through.
The times you're in need, and the happy times too!

They can sometimes seem mean, but mostly kind.
As it's always your best interests, that they have in mind.

You know that they'd never hurt you, that is true.
For you see the love they have, to give you through and through.

You don't always like, what they have to say.
Just open your mind, don't push them away.

They help you through, the days you cannot cope.
They fill your days, with love and hope.

So if you wonder, what a true friend will do.
Just ask me, as I have a few!

God's Will

What do we all fear, the most thus far?
Is it who we were, or who we are?

It really is, so plain to see,
Take it one day at time, to keep us free.

Stop living in the past, and tomorrow is not here.
Just live for today, to stop all of that fear.

Go on with life, stride by stride.
And we will find, we have nothing to hide.

It may take awhile, for us to find the way.
If we find it difficult, just stop and say…

"Thy will, not mine be done!"
Doing it our way, we will always run.

We run away, from the life chose for us.
It will happen, we need not rush!

Growing Faith

When you feel frustrated, and lost your way.
Ask for God's help, as you quietly pray.

Now just let go, and you will receive.
Our faith grows stronger, when we start to believe.

Ask for the knowledge of God's will, and the power to carry it out.
As you will start to feel, what true faith is about.

So never give up, and your faith will grow.
Accepting that sometimes it's fast, and sometimes it's slow.

Open Up

When we were younger, it was hard to see.
What the future held, and where and what we would be.

But as we grew older, it started to become clear.
The only thing holding us back, was our own inner fear.

So day by day, we would see the light.
We stopped denying, and stopped the fight.

Sometimes we need others, to help point it out.
If we just dig deep, we find what it's all been about,

When we close our minds, to what we could be.
We close our hearts, to the chance to be free.

So if we open our mind, which will open our heart.
We find each and every day, to be a fresh new start!

Live To Be Free

Life is to short, to throw it away,
To sit and procrastinate, day by day.

Finding excuses, you will always do,
Instead look for what could be, right in front of you.

Get rid of the fear, get rid of the pain.
Take the time, to dance in the rain.

Go enjoy, leave your worries behind,
After all, it's happiness you may find.

Do the things, that you want to do,
Enjoy every moment, that's the best thing for you.

So lighten up, and live for today,
Then tomorrow, "Thanks for yesterday," is what you will say.

What's the worst, that could happen to you?
You open up, to what could be new.

Do this each day, and life will be,
Simple steps, to setting you free!

You Will Get Through

Some lessons in life, can really be rough.
They can bring you down, until you''ve had enough.

That's when you need, to choose to let go.
As hard as it is, to go with the flow.

The sadness, self-pity, and all of the pain,
Once overcome, it's what you will gain.

Each one you get through, the stronger you feel.
As long as you stop running, on your self-will.

At the end of the tunnel, there is light.
It's there to see, when you stop the fight.

You have no control, over life's surprises.
But each day, that sun still rises.

So keep your chin up, and do not frown.
The world can't see you smile, when you're looking down!

True To You

Being honest with yourself, should be the first thing you do.
Honesty to others, will be a strong number two.

Kidding yourself, hiding behind a wall.
Does no good, except make you fall.

Hiding inside yourself, leads to dismay.
So open up, to help you find your way.

Thinking that everything in life, is not always fine.
Will just keep you falling, to the end of the line.

The more you release, the better you feel.
It may take awhile, but what's the big deal.

It's worth the risk, what's the worst it could do?
Make you happy, so be true to you!

Go For It

When you get over your fear, to experience something new.
You will be grateful it happened, as it will help you.

They don't always work out, but sometimes they do.
Either way, they become a part of you.

There is always a reason, why life happens this way.
It's to keep you searching, each and every day.

Whether it makes you happy, or makes you sad.
It will turn out to be, the best experience you've had.

So go ahead, and try something new,
You'll feel better inside, that much is true.

Close your eyes, and breath real deep.
Trust in yourself, to take that leap.

Pain

When something special, is taken from you,
It may make you feel, like you've been torn in two.

The pain can be, so extremely strong.
But why it was taken, was it right or wrong?

Feeling like there is, no surviving the pain,
But if you don't go through it, you'll have nothing to gain.

You believe that you, will never be able to feel,
The happiness inside, which this made seem so real.

You still have a life, when something is taken away.
The pain turns to growth, so you will be okay.

Thoughts

Some thoughts can take over, and mess you up.
Always wondering, "half full or half empty," in your cup.

If you allow yourself, to let the demons in,
You're risking the chance, that you will never win.

You can live your life, with your head in the ground.
Only to miss out, on what could be found,

So take your head out, and look around you.
There is peace, freedom and happiness too!

Those crazy thoughts, do not have to run the show.
Use your strength within, so you can let them go.

Then each day, can get alittle brighter,
And each load, will become alittle lighter.

Who You Were

Oh how selfish, we can be,
When we do not look, at what we need to see.

When it's all about you, caring nothing at all,
About feelings of others, as you make them so small.

But once you realize, and it may be too late.
Then all you are left with, is your own self-hate.

You loose respect for yourself, whatever you had.
But loosing it from others, could drive you mad.

It's hard to be, the person you want to be.
When the person you were, is all you can see!

The RollerCoaster

Lifes' journey, can be one big surprise.
There are things that happen, to open your eyes

Each time you get off, you begin to see,
That each ride seems shorter, as more troubles flee.

Don't get stuck on it, because you're full of fear.
Make it time to get off, and get your life in gear.

Yes the RollerCoaster, can be quite a ride.
Only you can stop it, when you get honest inside.

Feelings

When you hold feelings inside, and don't let them flow,
The pain grows so deep, that you will need to let go.

You need to release them, and go through the pain.
The only alternative, is to go slowly insane.

If you accept them, release them, and then let them go.
You will be amazed, at how much you actually grow.

Being honest with your feelings, clears the way,
To happiness and peace, each and every day.

So for today, just be the best you can be.
All will balance in time, you wait and see.

To Let Go

The hardest part, of letting go,
Is knowing you have to, but feeling so low.

The pain is so intense, you'd rather die.
But to push through, go ahead and cry.

Letting go, will set you free.
Then all that pain, becomes history.

The longer you hold on, the harder it gets.
Leaving it inside, should not be where it sits

The feelings and emotions, keep hitting you.
When you're in so deep, what can you do?

Get down on your knees, and say a prayer
To let it all go, so you can start to care.

Crazy thoughts, will run through your mind.
They take over, but if you seek you will find.

Those squirrels, don't have to run so free.
Chase them out, so what will be will be.

Surrender

How long do you let it go on, eating you up inside?
When you can get the strength, to carry on with pride.

Surrender it all, every day until it's lifted,
What you're left with, is a feeling of being gifted.

It will take patience, and time to get there.
Knowing that you will, makes you aware.

Just hand it over, to get rid of it.
Then enjoy life, as your eyes are lit.

Surrendering, will get you through,
That which you thought, you could not do.

Lighten up, laugh and smile.
Because you've just gone, another mile.

Wait

You can move the world, if you're ready to roll.
Why give up, and stick your head in a hole.

Why make your life miserable, when you can do it with ease.
Then you can see the trees through the forest, not the forest through the trees.

Denying, hiding and running from it all.
Is you choosing, to keep hitting that wall.

You have to have faith, to get through the day.
Always letting it slip, leads you the wrong way.

Patience will help, you just have to wait.
Good things will happen, it's never too late.

Get Over It

You sit and feel sorry for youself, thinking life's done you harm.
In actual fact, it was you who set off the alarm.

You drag yourself down, and other people too.
Snap out of it, life goes on, as should you.

Get over yourself, and out of your head.
So you don't leave yourself, hanging by a thread.

Have some faith, go ahead and jump.
If you ever want, to get over that hump.

Don't dwell on the past, as it's now gone.
Put a smile on your face, and just move on.

Always Be Grateful

There are so many things, that you forget.
That made you grateful, when they hit.

Our life gets so cluttered, it takes that away.
Still always show gratitude, each and every day.

It's those things to be grateful for, which make us whole.
When forgotten, that's when it takes its toll.

So remember to make, a list every night.
Of the things in your day, that give you delight.

Direction

The sky's the limit, if you just stop and see.
There is a whole world out there, that's the key.

When you find your direction, and you will.
It could take time, but you'll get up that hill.

Don't let distractions, get in the way.
Strength will help, so your focus won't stray.

Don't look back at a life, you thought you lost.
You deserve to ge happy, at any cost.

The Past

The years of struggles, you put yourself through.
Are now the past, which leaves your life up to you.

It took opening your mind, and opening your eyes.
You had to go through it, the past makes you wise.

Life is wonderful, once you look at the way,
The road brought you here, living in today.

So live this life, the best way you know how.
The past is the past, and the present is now.

Ride The Wave

Be good to yourself, don't let that slip.
Push yourself forward, keep a firm upper lip.

If you're feeling down, find your belief.
Once you do, you'll feel a sigh of relief.

You feel better about yourself, knowing you care.
Life goes much smoother, when you treat yourself fair.

So get on that surfboard, and ride the wave.
As this is your life, you are choosing to save.

Humble

So I lived in denial, for so many years.
To escape my inner, and outer fears.

I'd put on my security blanket, day by day,
Convinced that my life, was truly God's way.

It took a push, more like a slap in the face.
To put my denial, finally in its place.

So I got humble, and honest inside,
And asked God to help, as I got on this ride.

The pain hit hard, but it had to be done.
Sometimes I'd walk through it, and sometimes I'd run.

My heart felt heavy, and torn apart,
Questioning if the honesty, was actually smart.

I now know, when things are a want not a need.
So I am cleaning my garden, weed by weed.

Through all the pain, I knew getting humble was right.
It was my denial, which knocked that clear out of sight.

I would get through it, as I brought it on.
To move on with my life, this had to be gone.

Finding Me

For too long, I had closed my eyes
Not seeing that my life, was one big disguise.

I'd shut everyone out, and kept to myself.
Placing my life to live, upon a shelf.

I convinced myself, that I was happy inside.
When all along, finding true happiness had died.

I didn't want to see, how I stopped living.
I was too busy holding onto, what I thought was giving.

I did not see, what it was doing to me.
Not aware, that I was loosing my identity.

I could never say no, but feeling regret.
Holding onto, all that denial yet.

Now I have no choice, but to help myself grow.
Caring for me, so I have something to show.

I felt responsible, for helping everyone.
Helping myself, should of been what I had done.

So now I sit wondering, why I was blind.
To the denial, I let take over my mind.

I became painfully aware, of how my life was meant to be.
So now I am strong, and regaining my identity.

Determination

The more life pulls me, the harder I push.
To come out from inside, that burning bush.

I let my strength inside, take control.
Then determination, fills my soul.

I don't give up on myself, when I believe life's done me wrong.
My determination, keeps me moving along.

If I allow myself, to stop and freeze.
The life that I strive for, would be gone in a breeze.

My determination, keeps me moving ahead.
So anything life throws at me, I have nothing to dread.

Insanity

I need to give myself time, to get through the pain.
Brought on by avoidance, which nearly drove me insane.

I looked at my world, through a cloudy haze.
Living in a fantasy, throughout the days.

When I finally realized, how I was living.
It became time, for the act of forgiving.

I stopped beating myself up, and put on a smile.
Then insanity lost out, mile after mile.

Vision of Me

The vision of me, is simple to see.
One of happiness, which is inside of me.

My goals, my purpose, my whole new look.
Comes from within me, the next chapter in my book.

There is nothing to stop me, from reaching my goal.
My open-mindedness, helped strengthen my soul.

I am stronger, more confident, and feeling free.
What I thought was taken, I have restored in me.

The past shut me down, and left me lost.
My new way of thinking, will recover the cost.

More Revealed

Going through life, thinking I knew everything.
I was more like a bird, with a broken wing.

All the pains I endured, I was at the end of the rope.
When in fact, day by day, they were bringing me hope.

I closed the door, on that which I denied.
In my subconscious, is where they would hide.

But they worked their way out, from deep inside.
Bringing new light to my life, on this amazing ride.

A ride of pain and tears, which welcomed peace.
As the road narrowed, I felt the release.

My subconscious, is like a package sealed.
But once opened, more is revealed.

The Road

As I travel along, the road ahead.
I know in my heart, I have nothing to dread.

As the road, leads the way,
To move ahead, day by day.

The road can be smooth, the road can be rough.
It's those potholes I hit, that make me tough.

I look behind, to see the distance I've gone.
The distance ahead, keeps me carrying on.

www.ingramcontent.com/pod-product-compliance
Lightning Source LLC
LaVergne TN
LVHW021742060526
838200LV00052B/3426